KU-327-566

THE ROMANS

ARE COMING!

Paul Mason

Illustrated by Martin Bustamante

W

FRANKLIN WATTS

LONDON•SYDNEY

Leabharlanna Poiblí Chathair Bhaile Átha Cliath

Dublin City Public Libraries

Franklin Watts
First published in Great Britain in 2018 by
The Watts Publishing Group
Copyright © The Watts Publishing
Group 2018

All rights reserved.

Credits
Series Editor: Julia Bird
Illustrator: Martin Bustamante
Packaged by: Collaborate Agency

ISBN 978 1 4451 5616 3

Image Credits
p.2 tl: © Bukhta Yurii/Shutterstock.com. p.3 br: © Bukhta Yurii/Shutterstock.com. p.4 bl: © View Apart/
Shutterstock.com. p.5 tr: © Viacheslav Lopatin/Shutterstock.com. p.5 bl: Following Hadrian/© Wikimedia
Commons. p.7 tr: © Bukhta Yurii/Shutterstock.com. p.7 br: © eFesenko/Shutterstock.com. p.9 tr: Interfoto/
Alamy. p.11 tr: © Photosampler/Shutterstock.com. p.11 bl: © C Jones/Shutterstock.com. p.12 bl: © Matei
Ionut/Shutterstock.com. p.13 tr: Matthias Kabel/© Wikimedia Commons. p.17 br: © David Peter Robinson/
Shutterstock.com. p.19 tr: © Massimo Salesi/Shutterstock.com. p.19 bl: De Agostini/Getty Images. p.21
tr: © Jay75/Shutterstock.com. p.23 br: © Kiev.Victor/Shutterstock.com. p.25 br: © bensliman hassan/
Shutterstock.com. p.27 cr: © Bertrand Benoit/Shutterstock.com. p.28 tr: © yahiyat/Shutterstock.com. p.28
br: © Laurence Gough/Shutterstock.com. p.29 br: © Yaroslaff/Shutterstock.com

Every attempt has been made to clear copyright.
Should there be any inadvertent omission please
apply to the publisher for rectification.

Franklin Watts
An imprint of
Hachette Children's Group
Part of The Watts Publishing Group
Carmelite House
50 Victoria Embankment
London EC4Y 0DZ

An Hachette UK Company
www.hachette.co.uk
www.franklinwatts.co.uk

Printed in China

MIX
Paper from
responsible sources
FSC® C104740
FSC
www.fsc.org

CONTENTS

Words in **bold** are
in the glossary
on page 30.

THE ROMANS

The city of Rome was **founded** in 753 BCE. Over the next centuries, Rome's power grew and grew. Eventually, it controlled the greatest empire ever seen.

Kings and republics

In the beginning, Rome was ruled by kings. But the seventh king, Tarquin, was a cruel and unpopular ruler. He was overthrown in 509 BCE and Rome became a **republic**, with rulers chosen by its people. The Republic fought many wars to gain territory. By around 275 BCE it controlled the whole of Italy. Rome then fought the great North African city of Carthage and won. By 146 BCE Rome controlled Sicily, the western Mediterranean, most of Spain and part of North Africa. The Romans also fought their way east into Asia.

EUROPE

= Roman Empire

ITALY

Rome

AFRICA

ASIA

By the 1st century BCE, Rome controlled most of Europe, North Africa and parts of Asia.

Dictators and empires

In 44 BCE, a Roman general named Julius Caesar was named **Dictator** of Rome. Caesar was popular because of his great military victories. He had beaten the rebellious **Gauls** in France and led an expedition to Britain, though he soon left again. However, a month after he became dictator, Caesar was murdered. By 27 BCE his heir, Octavian, had fought his way to power. The title 'dictator' had been abolished after Caesar's murder – Octavian was named 'emperor' instead. For the next 500 years, emperors ruled Rome.

A statue of Julius Caesar, who led the first Roman expedition to Britain.

The Romans in Britain

In CE 43 the Roman army returned to Britain, apparently with the aim of seizing Britain's precious metals. In reality, though, the Romans came because the new emperor, Claudius, told them to. Claudius was worried: some of Rome's territories were under attack. People might hold Claudius responsible. **Conquering** a new land would make him more popular.

Imagine what it must have been like for the Britons, once they realised that the Romans were coming …

Emperor Claudius ruled Rome from CE 41 to 54.

HOW DO WE KNOW?

According to legend, Rome was founded by twin brothers, Romulus and Remus. The two could not agree where Rome should be located. They fought, and Romulus killed Remus.

No one is sure where this story comes from, and it is unlikely to be true. But it was important to the Romans, and they left evidence of it wherever they went.

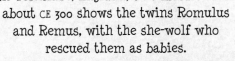
In Yorkshire, England, this **mosaic** from about CE 300 shows the twins Romulus and Remus, with the she-wolf who rescued them as babies.

THE ROMANS ARE COMING!

Early today we heard that a fleet of ships had been
seen off the coast, so we rushed to investigate.
The rumours were true. The Romans are back!

CHIEF VERICA V. CHIEF CARATACUS

This all started with an argument between two of our British chiefs.
Chief Verica was pushed out of his lands by Chief Caratacus. But
Verica's dad had been put in charge by Caesar, the last time the
Romans were here. Verica sent a message to Rome, asking for help.

Now a fleet of ships is arriving in Kent, loaded with soldiers, luggage
and nasty weapons. Some of our warriors went to try to persuade
the Romans to leave – but hardly any returned.

It looks as though we're being invaded.
We Britons are going to have to get used
to having the Romans around.

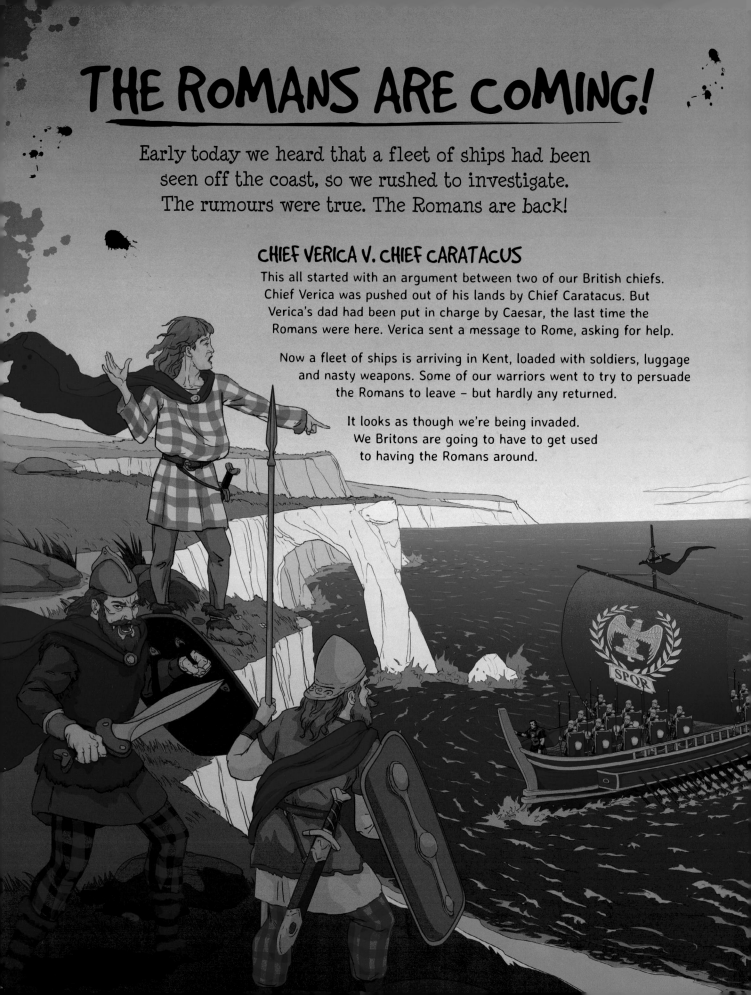

So, what are the Romans like?

The Romans can be a bit touchy. As they tend to solve arguments by burning down your whole village and forcing everyone into **slavery,** it is worth knowing how to get along with them. What my fellow Britons need is a bit of help understanding what's coming their way.

Fortunately, people from my family have been to Gaul – which the Romans basically own – many times, to trade goods or earn money fighting for the local chiefs. We know a lot about the Romans: how they fight and live, their customs and what kind of rulers they are.

Coins from ancient Gaul have been found in southern England. They show that there was trade between the two countries long before the Romans arrived.

This mosaic shows Roman ships on their way to Britain.

HOW DO WE KNOW?

How do we know what Roman Britain was like? We get evidence from a variety of **sources.**

First, the Romans left behind written records. Diaries, letters, official reports and **tax** records all give us information.

The Romans also left behind **archaeological** evidence. Their buildings, jewellery, cooking equipment and weapons all help us understand the Roman world.

THE ROMAN ARMY

The first thing that's going to be coming our way is the Roman army. This isn't usually a reason for celebration ... unless it's a funeral celebration. If they plan on fighting the Romans, the British warriors will need to learn quickly how the Roman army is run.

ORGANISATION

The basic unit of the Roman army is called a 'century'. A century contains about 80 soldiers, led by a centurion. Each century trains and fights together. The next layer is a 'cohort'. This is made up of six centuries, so it has about 500 soldiers. Take ten cohorts and you have a 'legion' of about 5,000 soldiers.

There are 30 legions in the Roman army: about 150,000 soldiers in total. Thank goodness they're not ALL coming to Britain.

TACTICS

The Romans don't fight like Britons. British warriors fight for their own honour and glory. Some strip off and paint themselves blue before battle. They look very fierce – but blue paint does not protect you as well as the metal armour the Romans wear!

The Romans also fight as a group. In battle they move slowly forward behind their wood-and-metal shields, all together in formation. When they get close enough, they start stabbing at you with their short swords.

CHARIOTS

The invaders have nothing like our fast-moving war chariots, though. The last time the Romans were here, the charioteers almost pushed them back into the sea! This time, they have learned their lesson. Almost the first thing the Romans did was **maim** Chief Caratacus' chariot horses in a night raid.

An engraving of the great Roman historian Dio (c.150–235).

HOW DO WE KNOW?

Some of our information about Rome's invasion of Britain comes from a Roman historian called Dio. During the early 200s, Dio wrote 80 books about the history of Rome. Dio's books were written over 150 years after the invasion happened. They also tell the story from a Roman viewpoint. As a result, Dio's information is not always 100 per cent reliable.

LEGIONARIES

Rome's legionaries are its top soldiers. To be a legionary you have to be:

- a man
- a Roman **citizen**
- at least 17 years old.

You also have to be pretty tough.

ROME'S ELITE

To be honest, the legionaries are a nightmare to fight. They are the Roman army's crack troops. Their lives are completely different from a British warrior's. The legionaries spend almost all their time together. They train together, live together, march together and do battle side-by-side. They fight in the same way and use the same equipment.

Metal helmet

Armour made of metal plates, linked together by leather straps

Wool tunic underneath armour

Dagger worn on the left-hand side

Javelin (a throwing spear)

Short sword, known as a *gladius*, worn on the right-hand side

Long, thick leather strips protect the upper leg. The strips are weighted at the end to stay in place.

Shield, held by the left arm, is made of thick wood wrapped in leather, with metal bands at the top and bottom

LEGIONARY TRAINING

Legionaries really never stop training. They keep fit by running, marching and practising their combat skills. They have to be able to march 30 km a day carrying all their kit and wearing armour. Legionaries can swim across rivers, build a road or a fort and smash their way into a stronghold.

Ask a British warrior to build you a road and he wouldn't even know what you were talking about: there ARE no roads in Britain.

FIGHTING STYLE

Legionaries usually attack by marching towards you in lines. They have their shields facing you. If your archers attack, the men behind lift their shields over their heads for protection. Then when they are close enough, the legionaries start stabbing you through gaps in the shield wall, or from beneath it.

Roman soldiers painted their shields in patterns representing their unit. They also included personal designs.

Maiden Castle is a huge hill fort. It was mostly built during the 1st century BCE and is believed to have been stormed by the Romans during their invasion.

HOW DO WE KNOW?

The Roman army left behind all kinds of information that can be dug up today. Maiden Castle in Dorset, for example, was a stronghold of the Britons. Archaeologists have found **artillery bolts** there, showing us some of the weapons the Romans used to attack the stronghold.

In many other places, Roman armour, swords and other weapons have been discovered.

AUXILIARY SOLDIERS

Only Roman citizens can become legionaries, but any man can join the Roman army, and many auxiliaries come from Rome's conquered lands. There are benefits to joining, but there are definitely bad points, too.

GOOD POINTS

You might not have a choice about joining the army! Sometimes the Romans just grab you and that's that. Even so, the army isn't all bad. Here are three good things about being an auxiliary:

1. **You get to see the world**
   As part of the Roman army, you might be sent anywhere in the Empire, as well as to soon-to-be parts of the Empire.

2. **You get regular wages, food, etc.**
   Every part of the Roman Empire has to pay taxes – and a big part of those taxes is spent on the Roman army. Becoming an auxiliary means some of that tax money will be spent on you!

3. **You become a Roman citizen**
   Roman citizens have special rights throughout the Empire. Retired soldiers may also get an area of land of their own to farm.

Roman ruins in the old province of Dacia, (now Romania) where retired soldiers were given land in the early 100s.

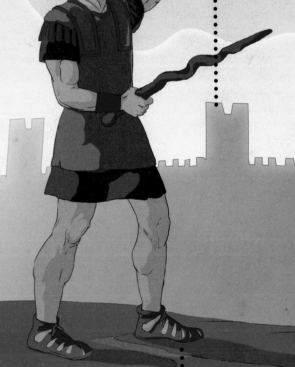

Auxiliaries spend most of their time training.

When they stop marching, the soldiers often have to build a temporary fort for the night.

They may have to march 30 km a day, carrying all their kit.

BAD POINTS

Not-so-good things about being an auxiliary:

1. Severe risk of death
Roman generals prefer to get auxiliaries killed instead of losing highly trained legionaries, so auxiliaries often get thrown into the worst fighting, where the risk of death or injury is highest.

2. You do not earn much
Despite the high risk of death, auxiliaries get paid only about a third as much as legionaries.

3. It takes ages to become a citizen
Once you join, you have to stay in the army for 25 years. Join at 17 (the minimum age) and you will be 42 when you retire – if you live that long!

HOW DO WE KNOW?

We know that auxiliaries became citizens because of bronze plates the Romans left behind. These are called 'diplomas' – part of one is shown here:

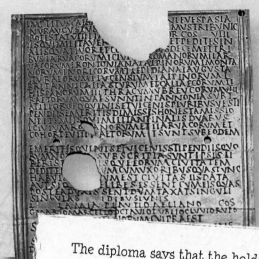

The diploma says that the holder has left the army with honour, and is now a Roman citizen.

THE ROMANS SPREAD OUT

Not all Britons will be making the Romans welcome. As soon as they realise not everyone is pleased to see them, the Roman soldiers will start building temporary forts each night for safety.

QUICKFIRE FORTS

It seems a lot of work to build a fort for a night or two. British warriors just set up camp and post a few sentries!

The temporary forts are called marching camps. Roman soldiers can build one in a few hours. They always build them in the same way.

The fort has four sides, made up of a deep ditch with the earth piled up inside to make a barrier. The barrier is made harder to attack by putting spikes, **palisades** or other defences on top.

Inside a marching camp there are three main areas.

1. The commanding officer's tent goes right in the middle, so that he's surrounded by defenders. The supplies and transport are usually kept here too.

14

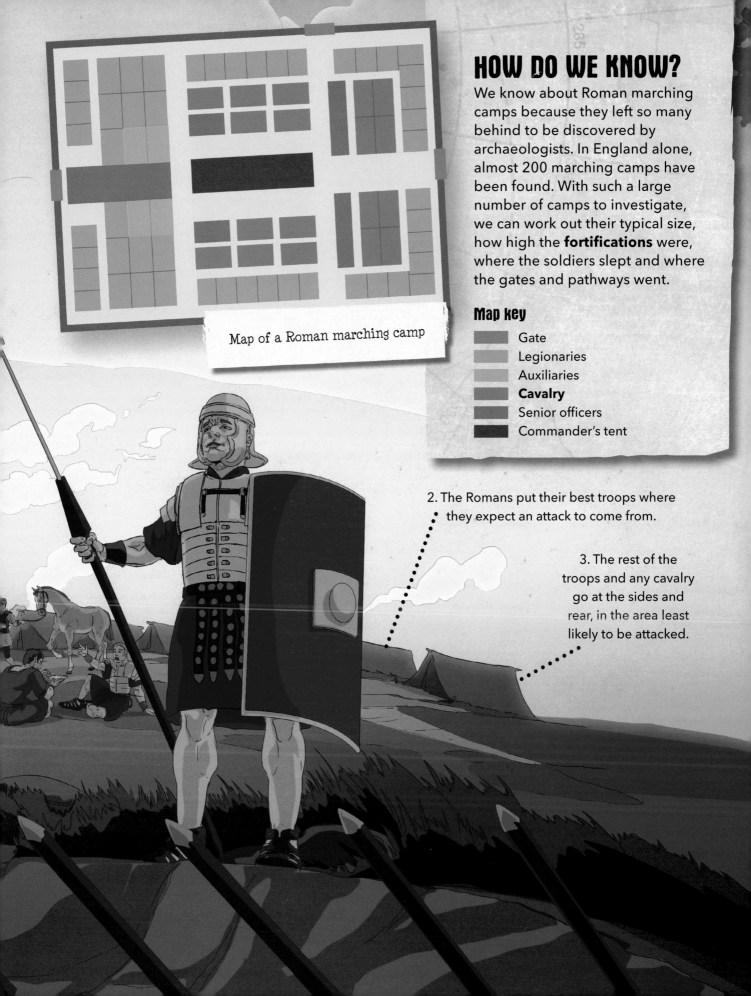

Map of a Roman marching camp

HOW DO WE KNOW?

We know about Roman marching camps because they left so many behind to be discovered by archaeologists. In England alone, almost 200 marching camps have been found. With such a large number of camps to investigate, we can work out their typical size, how high the **fortifications** were, where the soldiers slept and where the gates and pathways went.

Map key

Gate
Legionaries
Auxiliaries
Cavalry
Senior officers
Commander's tent

2. The Romans put their best troops where they expect an attack to come from.

3. The rest of the troops and any cavalry go at the sides and rear, in the area least likely to be attacked.

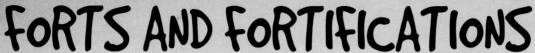

FORTS AND FORTIFICATIONS

Once the Romans have control in an area, they build proper forts. These forts are a real headache to attack! You CAN sometimes fight your way into a Roman fort. The trouble is, by the time you get in, you usually leave a trail of dead or wounded fellow warriors behind you.

FEARSOME FORTS

Auxiliary forts are a bigger, better version of marching camps. The walls are usually made of turf and earth, with a wooden **rampart** on top. There is a guard tower on each corner. It's hard to sneak up on these towers. Roman sentries are put to death for falling asleep on duty, so they are ALWAYS awake and watching.

Inside an auxiliary fort there are proper buildings, mostly made of wood. The main building at the centre is usually made of stone.

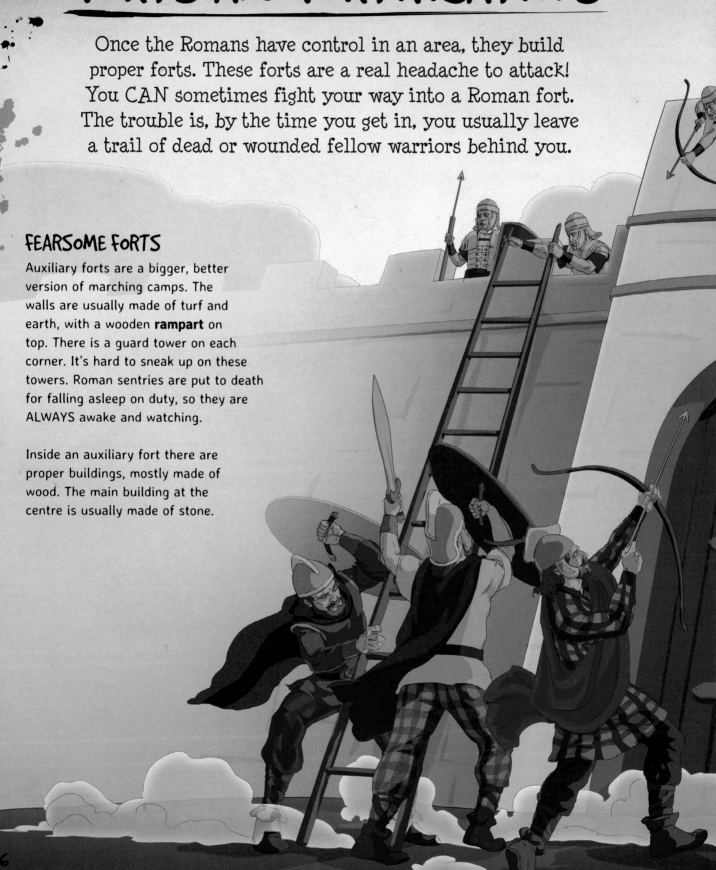

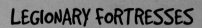

LEGIONARY FORTRESSES

The biggest fortresses are designed to fit a whole legion – about 5,000 legionaries. These take even the Romans a long time to build! The walls are almost always made of stone, and the buildings inside are a mixture of stone and wood.

Once the Romans get these massive fortresses built, they are not going anywhere soon. The legionary forts make it easier for the Romans to control whole areas. If danger threatens, they just disappear inside and dare you to attack. Then, when reinforcements arrive, they emerge ... and start taking their revenge.

The castle at Portchester was built during the 12th century. The outer walls were made by the Romans, a thousand years earlier.

HOW DO WE KNOW?

The Romans built forts everywhere they went. The forts were so well built that elements of some of them survive even today. One of the best Roman forts in Britain is Portchester Castle, near Portsmouth. The outer walls of the castle are as the Romans built them. The walls stayed so secure that after the Napoleonic Wars (1803–1815) the fort was used as a prisoner-of-war camp.

ROAD BUILDING

The Romans are famous across Europe for their road-building skills. At the moment in Britain all we have is cart tracks – but that could all be about to change.

WHAT ROMAN ROADS MEAN FOR BRITAIN – PART 1

When the Romans start building roads, any British resistance will really be in trouble. Most Roman roads are built by the army. Other people can use them, but when the army is coming through, you have to get out of the way. This means the soldiers can reach trouble spots and crush uprisings really quickly.

WHAT ROMAN ROADS MEAN FOR BRITAIN – PART 2

Roman roads could actually be one good thing to come out of the invasion. They will let people travel more easily. Getting goods to market – or even to one of the towns the Romans are bound to start building soon - is going to be much faster.

HOW A ROMAN ROAD IS BUILT

Romans prefer a road to be straight. Their roads usually start life as a straight line, marked with a series of stakes. Parallel to the line, two ditches are dug. Earth and rocks from the ditches are piled up in the middle, so the road is higher than the surrounding ground. Clay, chalk or gravel go on top, then bigger, flat stones. The road is always higher in the middle than at the side so that water drains off it.

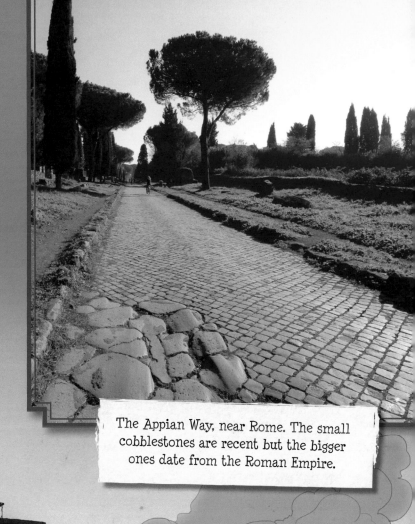

The Appian Way, near Rome. The small cobblestones are recent but the bigger ones date from the Roman Empire.

HOW DO WE KNOW?

We know how the Romans got their roads straight because of a tool called a *groma*. The groma was used to draw a straight line across the landscape. The **surveyor** lined up the front and rear strings in the direction the road would take. Then **stakes** were driven in along the line of the two strings.

The simple framework and weighted strings of a groma allowed Roman engineers to build the straightest roads the world had ever seen.

LIFE UNDER THE ROMANS

The Romans will crush any Britons who resist.
But if any of our chiefs agree to:

- be in the Empire
- obey Roman laws, and
- pay taxes

they'll get to keep their jobs.

VERCINGETORIX

If any chiefs are unsure whether to resist or not, they might like to think about Vercingetorix. He was a great chief among the Gauls. In 52 BCE he gathered together many tribes to fight the Roman general Julius Caesar (see page 4).

For a while the Gauls stopped Caesar from taking control of their country. By September of 52 BCE, though, Vercingetorix had been trapped in the city of Alesia. Surrounded by Caesar's army, he surrendered.

Vercingetorix was taken back to Rome in chains, put in prison and finally executed. His warriors were either killed or sold into slavery.

WHAT'S SO BAD ABOUT THE ROMANS, ANYWAY?

It's a bad idea to get on the wrong side of the Romans by not doing what they want. But that's true of our own chiefs, too! Britons might actually find there are quite a few advantages to having the Romans around.

Right now, for example, there is nothing in Britain quite like a Roman villa. They even have underfloor heating! A Roman bath is an amazing sight, too. Having one of those makes you realise you were never really clean before. In fact, there are a lot of things about the Romans that might just make life better.

A statue of Vercingetorix. After his surrender, he was taken to Rome and paraded through the streets, then strangled to death. It demonstrated what happened to anyone who resisted the Romans.

HOW DO WE KNOW?

There are two versions of the story of Vercingetorix. The first comes from Dio (see page 9). The second is from Caesar himself. Their versions are different. See if you can work out why that might be.

1. In Dio's version, Vercingetorix realises that he cannot win. He makes his way to Caesar's camp, where he appears suddenly and surrenders.

2. In Caesar's version, Vercingetorix does not choose to surrender. He is betrayed by the other Gaulish chiefs, who have realised they cannot win and hand him over to the Romans.

ROMAN TOWNS

Most Britons live in the countryside. Our towns – if you can call them that – are small, muddy, **ramshackle** places with wooden buildings. They are nothing like the kind of town the Romans build.

THE FORUM

In the middle of a Roman town there is a square called a forum, where they hold markets and other big events. Nearby will be the basilica, a big building where officials work and the **law courts** are held.

FINDING YOUR WAY

The town is laid out in a grid pattern. From the forum, streets always lead off in straight lines. Surrounding the town is a high stone wall to protect the town from attack.

THE BATHS

Most Roman towns have public baths. For a small amount of money, anyone can use them. These will be a BIG surprise to Britons!

First you strip off your clothes, and do some exercise to get sweaty. Then you go into the hot bath. Someone rubs oil into your skin, then scrapes it off with a tool called a *strigil*. The idea is that as you sweat, unhealthy things leave your body.

Once you've been scraped clean, you go into a warm bath, then a cold one, to cool down.

HOW DO WE KNOW?

Many places in Europe grew from Roman towns. London, Paris, Zurich and Barcelona, for example, all began in this way. Their Roman walls, and sometimes the street layout, can still be seen.

In Britain, anywhere with 'chester', 'caster' or 'cester' at the end of its name was probably a Roman town. These words all come from the Roman word *castrum*, which means fort.

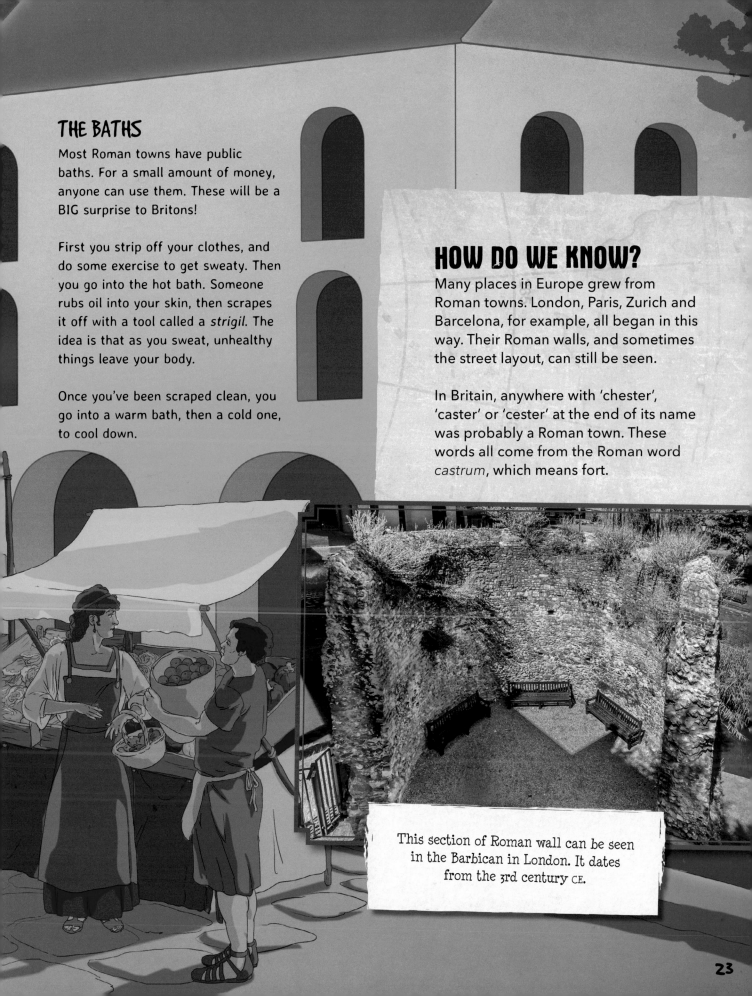

This section of Roman wall can be seen in the Barbican in London. It dates from the 3rd century CE.

ROMAN ENTERTAINMENT

Once the Romans build a town, it isn't long before they build an amphitheatre. This is where they go for entertainment, and sometimes religious ceremonies.

THEATRE

The Romans LOVE theatre. Some of their plays are quite rude, which will be popular with Britons. A lot of Roman plays, though, are a bit dull. The characters are usually very similar, and there is often a 'lesson' at the end.

GLADIATORS

One form of Roman entertainment Britons definitely WILL enjoy is gladiatorial contests. Gladiators are **slaves**, or sometimes criminals, forced to fight each other for the entertainment of the crowd. Gladiators come from every part of the Roman Empire.

If you're really good at fighting, being a gladiator isn't 100 per cent bad. True, you do kill people for a living, and there's a fairly big risk you will die yourself. But if you win enough victories, you might also win back your freedom.

The Romans like to make gladiatorial fights interesting. They often make a heavily armoured, slow-moving gladiator fight a light-armoured, fast one.

A retiarius gladiator fights with a net, plus either a trident or a dagger. He has little armour, but is fast-moving.

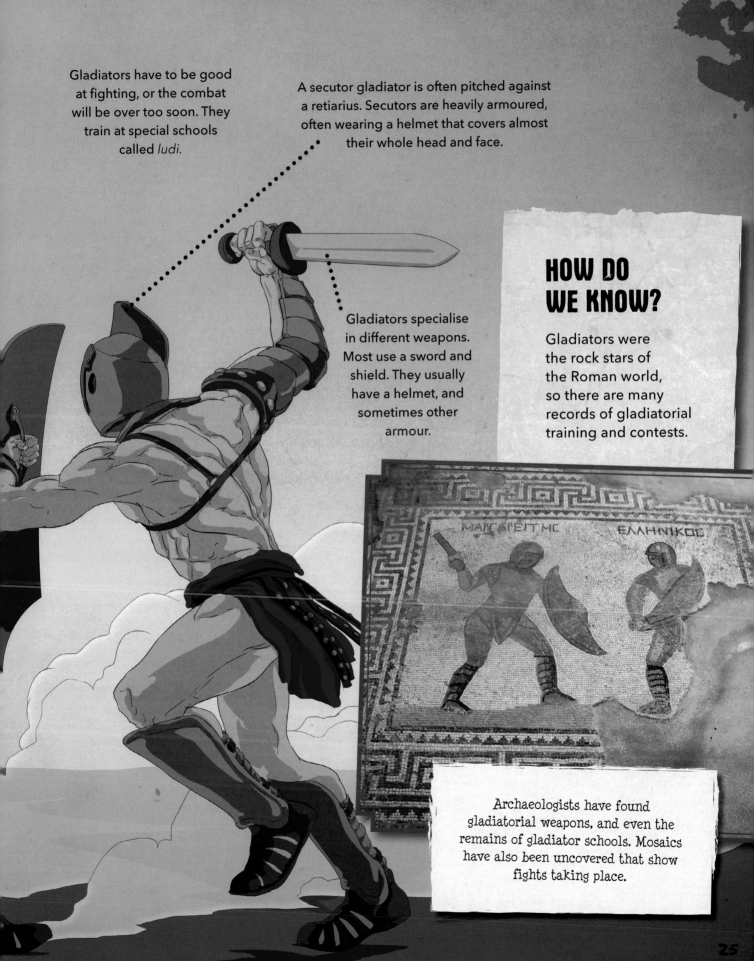

Gladiators have to be good at fighting, or the combat will be over too soon. They train at special schools called *ludi*.

A secutor gladiator is often pitched against a retiarius. Secutors are heavily armoured, often wearing a helmet that covers almost their whole head and face.

Gladiators specialise in different weapons. Most use a sword and shield. They usually have a helmet, and sometimes other armour.

HOW DO WE KNOW?

Gladiators were the rock stars of the Roman world, so there are many records of gladiatorial training and contests.

Archaeologists have found gladiatorial weapons, and even the remains of gladiator schools. Mosaics have also been uncovered that show fights taking place.

CRIME AND PUNISHMENT

Under Roman rule, any Britons who don't do as they are told will have to watch out. The Romans have a long list of crimes and punishments.

THREE KINDS OF CRIME

The Romans think there are three kinds of crime:

- Crimes against authority (i.e. the Romans)
- Crimes against the person (i.e. the Romans and a few other people)
- Crimes against property (which is usually owned by - you guessed it - the Romans).

Not everyone is equal under Roman law. Roman citizens are treated differently from non-citizens and slaves.

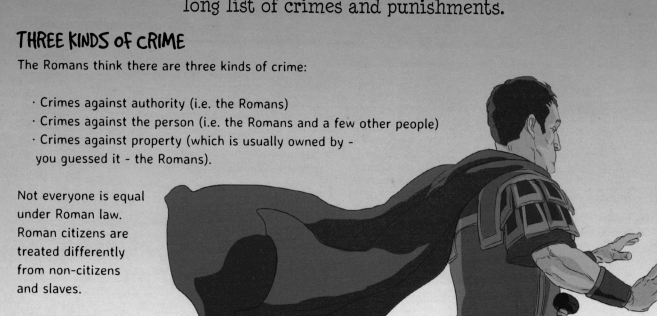

SLAVES V. NON-SLAVES

The Romans have a LOT of different punishments. They view slaves as valuable property, so slave punishments are unpleasant, but not always deadly. Slaves may be whipped or beaten, **branded** on the forehead, or forced to carry a heavy piece of wood around their neck for weeks or months. Particularly bad slaves are crucified.

For non-slaves, serious crimes are usually punished by death. The Romans are very imaginative about this. Their ways of executing criminals include:

· Cutting off their head
· Throwing them from a high place
· Strangling them
· Burying them alive.

The worst Roman punishment is for killing your father. You get sewn up in a sack, along with some hungry, angry animals. The Romans like to put in a snake, a dog and an ape. Then all four of you are thrown into a river to drown – if you don't get ripped apart first by terrified animals.

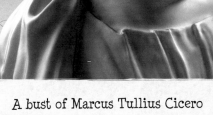

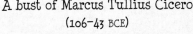
A bust of Marcus Tullius Cicero
(106–43 BCE)

HOW DO WE KNOW?

We know about punishments – and a lot of other details of Roman life – from the writings of Marcus Tullius Cicero.

Cicero was a famous Roman lawyer and politician. He was born in 106 BCE, and died in the year of Claudius's invasion of Britain, 43 BCE. Cicero's letters and other writings are the source for much of what we know about Roman life.

FALL OF THE EMPIRE

The Roman invasion of Britain succeeded. For 400 years Rome controlled territory all the way to Scotland. By the late 300s, though, the Roman Empire had grown too big and was crumbling. In 378, over 10,000 Roman soldiers were killed at the Battle of Adrianople. It was two-thirds of the whole Roman force.

The Romans and Britain

By the late 300s, the Romans could no longer keep control in Britain. In 410, the Roman Emperor Honorius wrote to the Britons:

'Fight bravely and defend your lives … you are now on your own.'

Army pay stopped reaching Britain, and the soldiers either left the army or returned to Rome. Any Romans wealthy enough to go home did. Britain was no longer part of the Empire.

Hadrian's Wall was built on the orders of the Emperor Hadrian, to keep warriors from the north out of Roman Britain.

After the Romans left, Britons avoided many places associated with them, leaving them untouched This mosaic was part of the floor of a grand Roman villa in Sussex that was rediscovered by a ploughman in 1811.

Legacy of the Romans

The Romans brought many new things to Britain. They built the first real towns, the first proper roads, stone-and-brick houses with underfloor heating, sewage systems and public baths. They also brought new animals, such as rabbits, and plants. We can thank the Romans for carrots and stinging nettles, for example. Stinging nettles were used by the Romans to treat some ailments.

New ideas also came to Britain from Rome. Christianity was a Roman import, though most Britons were not very keen on it at the time. Britons had their own gods, as well as priests called druids. The use of money was made popular, and the Romans taught Britons to read and write. Thousands of our words are based on Roman ones: *beast* (bestia), *decimal* (decimus) and *school* (schola) for example.

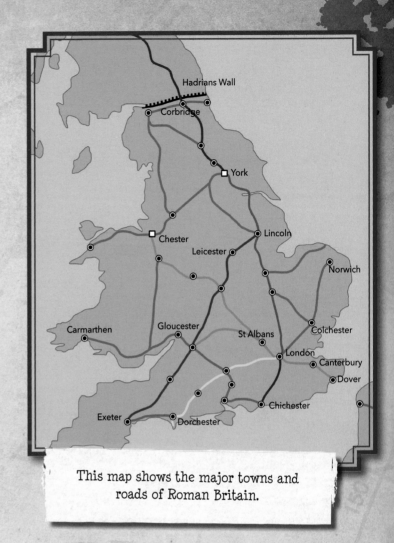

This map shows the major towns and roads of Roman Britain.

Fall of the Western Empire

In an attempt to save the vast Roman Empire, Emperor Theodosius I divided it into two halves in 395. The Western Empire was ruled from Rome, the Eastern Empire from the city of Constantinople (modern Istanbul).

Throughout the 400s, Rome was under attack from other European forces. The last Emperor, Romulus, was defeated and cast from power in 476. Rome's Eastern Empire lasted for almost another thousand years. The Western Empire, though, was gone. It became known as the Byzantine Empire.

HOW DO WE KNOW?

Army pay was the main way Roman coins found their way to Britain. Roman coins showed the emperor who was in power when they were made. Archaeologists have found almost no Roman coins from the early 400s. This suggests that by then, army pay had stopped arriving.

The Roman coin was found in England. It shows the head of Emperor Macrinus, which tells us that it was made between 217 and 218 CE.

GLOSSARY

archaeology   study of actual objects from ancient times

artillery   any kind of large weapon that can be used for long-distance attacks

BCE   short for 'Before Common Era', which refers to a date earlier than the year 0

bolt   short, heavy arrow fired from a crossbow

branded   burned with red-hot metal, in a way that leaves a permanent mark

cavalry   soldiers trained to fight on horseback

CE   short for 'Common Era', which refers to a date after the year 0

citizen   legal member of a country, who has the right to vote in elections

conquer   to take control of

dictator   ruler with complete power

fortification   wall or other structure (for example a tower) built for defending a place against attack

founded   begun (this word often describes an organisation, city or country)

Gaul   area of Europe that is today part of France

law court   place where criminals are tried and told their punishment

maim   cause physical damage that will last forever

mosaic   image made up of many tiny tiles of different colours

palisade   fence made of wooden stakes driven into the ground

rampart   part of the wall of a castle or fort, which has a walkway on top

ramshackle   badly organised and messy

republic   country where the leaders are voted into power

slave   person whose freedom has been taken away without cause and who is forced to work for someone else without payment

slavery   the condition of being a slave

source   place where something comes from, especially information

stake   wooden post with a pointed end, which can be hammered into the ground

surveyor   person who prepares a piece of land for building work

tactics   planned actions that are designed to get a particular result

tax   payment to the government

Glossary of Roman insults

The Romans were great at insulting each other. The Roman politician Petronius once told a rival:

'Curris, stupes, satagis, tanquam mus in matella', which in English means, 'All you do is run back and forth with a stupid expression, nervous as a rat in a roasting pot.' That's quite a lot to learn, though – so here are three shorter Roman insults:

Vescere bracis meis ('Eat my shorts', one for fans of *The Simpsons*)

Asinus asinum fricat ('The jackass rubs the jackass', a Roman way of describing someone sucking up to someone else)

Derideo te ('I laugh at you')

Timeline of Ancient Rome

753 BCE	**509** BCE	**44** BCE	**27** BCE	CE **30**	CE **43**
Rome is founded	Rome becomes a republic, ruled by elected politicians	Julius Caesar becomes Dictator, but is then assassinated by politicians who want to return to a republic	Octavian, Caesar's heir, becomes Emperor	Emperor Constantine allows Christians to worship freely	The Roman army invades England

FINDING OUT MORE

Roman sites

There are many Roman sites to visit around Britain. Two of the best are:

Fishbourne Roman Palace
Roman Way, Fishbourne
Chichester, West Sussex
PO19 3QR
England

The palace holds special events and exhibitions, including sometimes opportunities for children to spend some time doing an actual archaeological dig.

More information about the palace can be found here: sussexpast.co.uk/properties-to-discover/fishbourne-roman-palace

Hadrian's Wall

This is the wall marking the northernmost limit of Roman power. The wall stretched from Wallsend on the River Tyne in the east to Bowness-on-Solway in the west. Just seeing the wall is an amazing reminder of the Romans, but there are two places specially worth a visit:

Housesteads Fort, perched up on a high part of the wall, Housesteads is a great place for imagining what life must have been like in Britain for a Roman auxiliary from a sunny, warm land. You also get the chance to look into the oldest toilet you will ever see!

Vindolanda (www.vindolanda.com) is at the site of one of the most important forts along Hadrian's Wall. There is a museum about the Romans in Britain, as well as archaeological discoveries.

Books to read

Truth or Busted: The Fact or Fiction Behind the Romans Peter Hepplewhite (Wayland, 2018)

Did the Romans REALLY use warm gladiator blood as medicine? This is the place to find out! A collection of things you have heard (or maybe not) about the Romans – but are they true?

The Best (and Worst) Jobs in Ancient Rome Clive Gifford (Wayland, 2017)

Was the worst job in ancient Rome being a fuller? (That's someone who spends their day cleaning clothes by trampling them in a vat of wee, by the way.) Find out here!

Found! Roman Britain
Moira Butterfield (Franklin Watts, 2017)

A lot of our information about the Romans comes from things (buildings, structures and objects) they left behind. *Found! Roman Britain* looks at 13 amazing Roman finds and what they tell us – not only about the Romans, but also about what the Romans did for us.

CE 80
The Colosseum, the great stadium in the middle of Rome, is finished. A hundred days of games follow

CE 395
The Empire is divided into a Western Empire, ruled from Rome, and an Eastern one, ruled from Constantinople

CE 410
The Roman army leaves England

CE 476
Emperor Romulus is defeated and the Western Empire falls apart

CE 1453
Constantinople is captured by Ottoman Turks – the Byzantine Empire is defeated

INDEX